WEREWOLF LIFE CYCLES

by Noah Leatherland

BEARPORT PUBLISHING

Minneapolis, Minnesota

Credits

All images courtesy of Shutterstock.com. With thanks to Getty Images, Thinkstock Photo, and iStockphoto. Cover – Luca Lorenzelli, Dan Kosmayer, Sergio Photone, Here, Jakub Krechowicz, sociologas, wabeno. Recurring – Elizaveta Mironets, sociologas, wabeno. P1 – Luca Lorenzelli. 4–5 – gan chaonan, leolintang. 6–7 – e71lena, iobard. 8–9 – rudall30, MrNoe, Embrace of Beauty. 10–11 – Fernando Astasio Avila, Pheelings media. 12–13 – Sarah Holmlund, GSoul. 14–15 – S-BELOV, Alexander Sviridov. 16–17 – DanieleGay, GSoul. 18–19 – Obsidian Fantasy Studio, GSoul. 20–21 – Warm_Tail, AiiR. 22–23 – PhotoBarmaley, Robert Eastman, Daniel-Alvarez. 24–25 – Nenad.C, mythja, Cast Of Thousands. 26–27 – VladKK, Radu Razvan. 28–29 – Julya Livshits, Jukka Heinovirta, HWWO Stock. 30 – Mike Pellinni.

Bearport Publishing Company Product Development Team

President: Jen Jenson; Director of Product Development: Spencer Brinker; Managing Editor: Allison Juda; Associate Editor: Naomi Reich; Associate Editor: Tiana Tran; Art Director: Colin O'Dea; Designer: Kim Jones; Designer: Kayla Eggert; Product Development Assistant: Owen Hamlin

Library of Congress Cataloging-in-Publication Data is available at www.loc.gov or upon request from the publisher.

ISBN: 979-8-89232-057-3 (hardcover)
ISBN: 979-8-89232-531-8 (paperback)
ISBN: 979-8-89232-190-7 (ebook)

For more information, write to Bearport Publishing, 5357 Penn Avenue South, Minneapolis, MN 55419.

CONTENTS

WHAT IS A LIFE CYCLE?

Every living thing has a life cycle. Over this cycle, living things go through different steps where they grow and change. They may look different with each new step of the cycle.

Eventually, they die. Living things **reproduce** so the cycle carries on after they are gone. This is all a normal part of living.

But what about creatures that are **paranormal**? Surely these beings would have a beginning, middle, and end to life, too.

People often explain things they don't understand by telling stories. Sometimes, the stories have very strange creatures!

What would a werewolf life cycle be like? Let's imagine. . . .

WHAT IS A WEREWOLF?

There are many **legends** about half-human, half-animal creatures. For thousands of years, we have been telling stories about people who turn into wolves. These creatures are called werewolves.

The name *werewolf* comes from Old English words for man and wolf. A werewolf is said to be a human with a beastly secret. Sometimes, they turn into a wolf.

A werewolf looks just like a regular person most of the time. Everything changes during a full moon. Then, they grow fur and **transform** into something that looks like a mix of human and wolf.

Their face changes, adding a long **snout** with pointy teeth. A werewolf grows sharp, deadly claws. Perhaps scariest of all, some stories say the human loses control while in this wolf form.

Deadly teeth

A person who believes they are a wolf or other nonhuman animal has something called lycanthropy (lye-KAN-thruh-pee).

BECOMING A WOLF

There are a few ways people are said to become werewolves. Some stories say a person is born as one. Others tell tales of people turning into the beasts because they have done bad things.

Most often, legends say people are made into werewolves by other werewolves. How could this happen?

In some legends, a werewolf needs to bite someone in order to change them. Many sicknesses are spread through the blood and **saliva**, so this makes some sense.

Other stories say a simple scratch is enough to change a person. Maybe there is something on a werewolf's claws.

STARTING TO CHANGE

Many illnesses take a little while to make a person feel sick. So, after a bloody attack by a werewolf, the hurt person may feel completely fine.

They may even feel incredible. Wolves are powerful. If a person were to start taking on wolflike **traits**, they may get some of a wolf's strength. They could also become faster. But then the full moon rises.

The full moon is said to cause a werewolf's transformation. Wolves have much stronger senses than people. Noises could start to become painfully loud for a changing werewolf. Smells may be horribly strong.

A wolf can smell prey that is more than a mile (1.6 km) away.

A werewolf is supposed to be very hairy. So, a person turning into a werewolf would need to grow a lot of long, thick hair. This could be itchy.

THE FULLY TRANSFORMED WEREWOLF

Going from a human body into one that is part wolf would take some big changes.

A person's mouth and nose would need to grow a lot to become a snout like a wolf's. Inside their mouth, they would need to grow more teeth. The ones they had would have to become longer and sharper, too.

Wolves have smaller bodies than adult humans. However, wolves have bigger jaws and more teeth.

Their entire skeleton would need to change. In many stories, this is said to be very painful. Bones snap and heal into completely different shapes. The werewolf's skeleton becomes something between human and wolf.

Fully transformed werewolves are thought to be more like a beast than a person.

DIET

Just like a human, a werewolf would need to eat to grow and get stronger. However, a werewolf's diet is probably more like an animal's than a person's.

Wolves live in packs. Most often, these groups have 6 to 10 animals.

Wolves are excellent hunters. They are some of the deadliest **predators** in the world. They hunt in groups, taking down animals that are much larger than themselves.

Wolves eat mostly meat. They eat the majority of any creature they catch. Wolves leave behind little more than some tufts of hair and a few bones.

Legends say that werewolves are not picky eaters. They hunt whatever they can find, including humans. Some stories say werewolves have eaten entire villages.

HABITAT

Wolves live on every continent except South America and Antarctica. But a werewolf's **habitat** would depend on where the person lives in their human form.

It's possible that some werewolves could be worried about hurting someone when they transform. So, they could live very far from others. They might live near a forest to hide when they change.

In 1589, German serial killer Peter Stump was put to death for killing people and eating their bodies. He said he could change into a wolf.

In some stories, werewolves are evil. They want to harm others and make more werewolves. These werewolves could live in cities or towns with lots of people. That way, they would have plenty of people to attack when they change.

THE OLD WEREWOLF

Once the full moon sets, a werewolf is said to turn back into a human. They stay this way until the next full moon. Then, they turn into a werewolf again.

Some say a werewolf becomes more powerful every time it changes. They may grow much bigger. Their teeth and claws become longer, sharper, and more deadly.

Stories say there is no known **cure** for werewolves. They must change into a wolf form at every full moon. Some stories say it gets easier to gain control with every transformation.

In other stories, the opposite happens. They say there are some werewolves that cannot change back into humans. They are stuck as giant beasts for the rest of their lives.

PASSING ON
THE PROBLEM

For almost all predators, the urge to hunt is hard to fight. A werewolf would likely be the same. In their beast form, they would probably think of little else.

Most people or other animals would be easy targets for werewolves. They would stand little chance if the creature found them.

For many predators, hunting is an **instinct.** This means it happens without the animal having to think about it.

Those who manage to get away from a werewolf might not be as lucky as they first think. If the stories are to believed, even one small scratch is enough to turn a person into a werewolf.

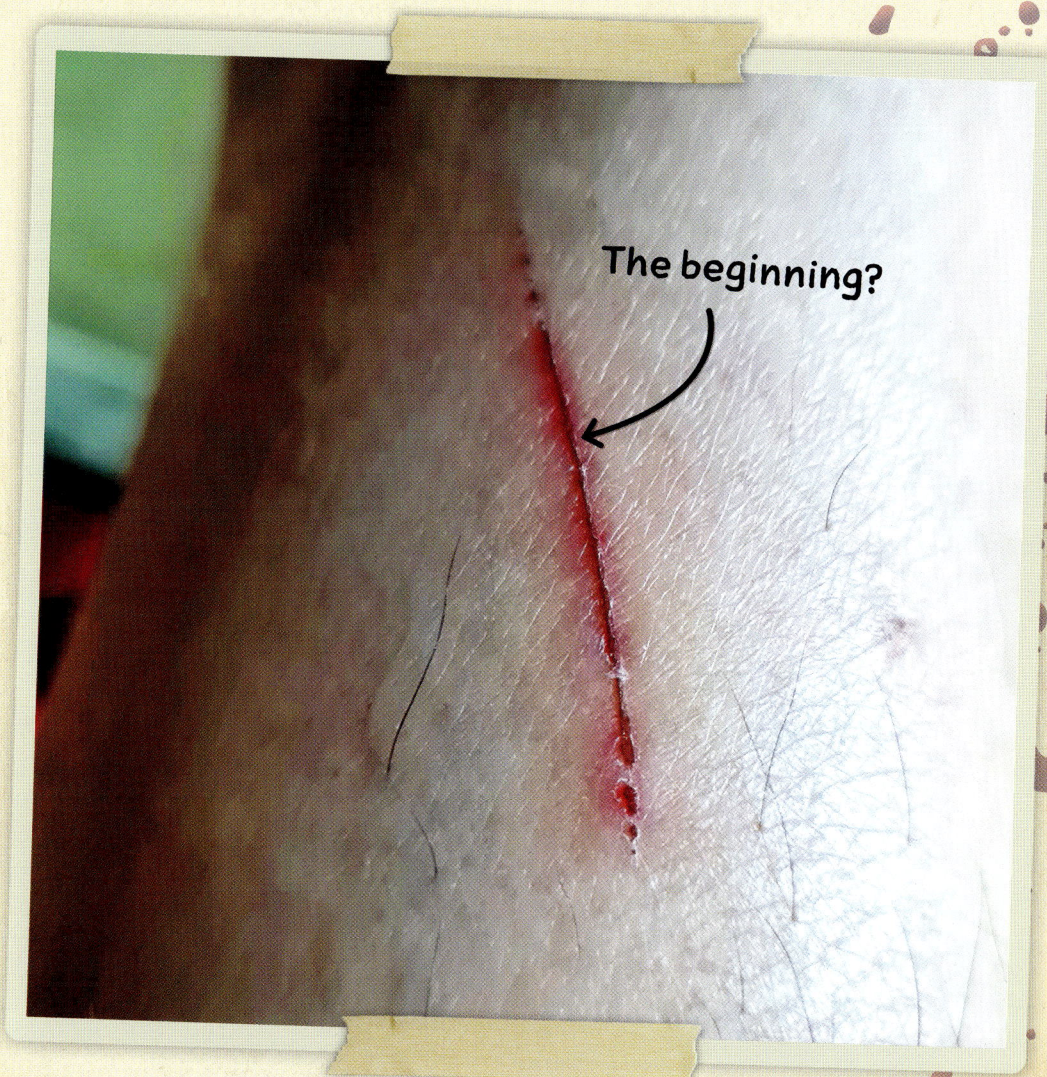

And just like that, the life cycle of the werewolf would continue.

OTHER WERE-CREATURES

In places where wolves are not common, stories tell of humans turning into other animals. The full moon is still what makes them change into their beastly forms.

WEREBEAR

Werebears are very similar to werewolves. They are humans that become a frightening grizzly bear when the moon is full.

Furry and frightening!

WERERABBIT

Some stories tell of people transforming into huge, scary versions of smaller animals. When someone is made into a wererabbit, it is said the full moon changes them into a giant rabbit monster.

In Ghana, there are not many wolves. Instead of werewolf stories, there are tales of people turning into hyenas.

SPOTTING A

WEREWOLF

If werewolves look like regular people most of the time, how might you spot one?

ACTING LIKE A DOG

A werewolf may keep some of their wolf traits even when in human form. They might chew on things as though they are bones. Be on the lookout for anyone strangely interested in smells.

In France between 1520 and 1630, there were more than 30,000 reports of people who appeared to be werewolves.

FULL MOON

The biggest clue would be what happens during a full moon. If this causes a transformation, it would be easy to spot a werewolf by how a person acts.

Do they hide when the full moon rises . . . and do you soon hear a wolf's howl in the distance?

HOW TO DEAL WITH
A WEREWOLF

If werewolves were real, they would be terrifying. But legends say there are a few things you can do to keep the beasts away.

SILVER

There are not many things that could hurt this powerful predator, but silver is said to be one of them. Silver burns werewolves.

So, keeping silver things around would stop werewolves from getting too close.

FLOWERS

If werewolves have a very good sense of smell, strong smells may be too much for them. Some stories say flowers are a good way to stop werewolves from getting too close.

Growing strong-smelling flowers around your home might just keep you safe.

One flower is said to have a strong affect on wolves. Wolfsbane has a **poison** that can kill wolves . . . and people!

LIFE CYCLE OF A

WEREWOLF

So, what might the life cycle of a werewolf look like? It could start with a scratch or a bite from another werewolf.

At first, the person may feel incredible . . . until the full moon comes out. Then, the transformation would start!

Their mouth and nose would stretch out into a wolf's snout. Fur would begin to grow all over their body. Their skeleton would shift and change, turning them into a werewolf!

The werewolf would scurry off into the night looking for a meal. If they come across an unlucky person, they might draw blood and make another werewolf . . . and so the cycle would continue.

Almost all living things grow, make young, and die. But a sea creature called the hydra can live forever. It doesn't age like other life on Earth.

BEWARE THE PARANORMAL!

There are stories around the world of all sorts of paranormal creatures. If you want to learn more, be very careful. . . .

Werewolves may be dangerous, but what if there is something even worse creeping around in the dark? How would their scary life cycle begin, continue, and end?

GLOSSARY

cure something that can be done to heal or treat a person who is sick

habitat a place in nature where a plant or animal normally lives

infected filled with harmful germs

instinct things an animal does or knows naturally, without having to learn

legends stories that are handed down from the past

paranormal things that are not able to be explained by science

poison something that can kill animals or people if eaten

predators animals that hunt and kill other animals for food

reproduce to make more of a living thing

saliva the liquid in the mouths of humans and other animals

snout the long front part of an animal's head that sticks out

traits qualities or characteristics of a person or other animal

transform to change into something else

INDEX

READ MORE

Huddleston, Emma. *Werewolves (Legendary Creatures).* Mankato, MN: The Child's World, 2022.

Troupe, Thomas Kingsley. *Werewolves (Mythical Creatures).* Minneapolis: Bellwether Media, 2021.

LEARN MORE ONLINE

1. Go to **www.factsurfer.com** or scan the QR code below.
2. Enter "**Werewolf Life Cycle**" into the search box.
3. Click on the cover of this book to see a list of websites.